W9-CMD-594

DISCARD

THE GREAT LAKES

The Great Lakes

BY JAMES P. BARRY

Illustrated with
photographs by the author

← A FIRST BOOK →

FRANKLIN WATTS | NEW YORK | LONDON | 1976

Photos courtesy of:
U.S. Army Corps of Engineers: pp. 5, 6;
Library of Congress: pp. 30–31;
U.S. Navy: p. 32.

Cover by Ginger Giles

Library of Congress Cataloging in Publication Data

Barry, James P
    The Great Lakes.

    (A First book)
    Includes index.
    SUMMARY: Discusses the history, economy, and
geography of the Great Lakes and surrounding
areas.
       1. Great Lakes—Juvenile literature. 2. Great
Lakes region—Juvenile literature. [1. Great Lakes.
2. Great Lakes region] I. Title.
F551.B38   977   76–15641
ISBN 0–531–00337–X

CONTENTS

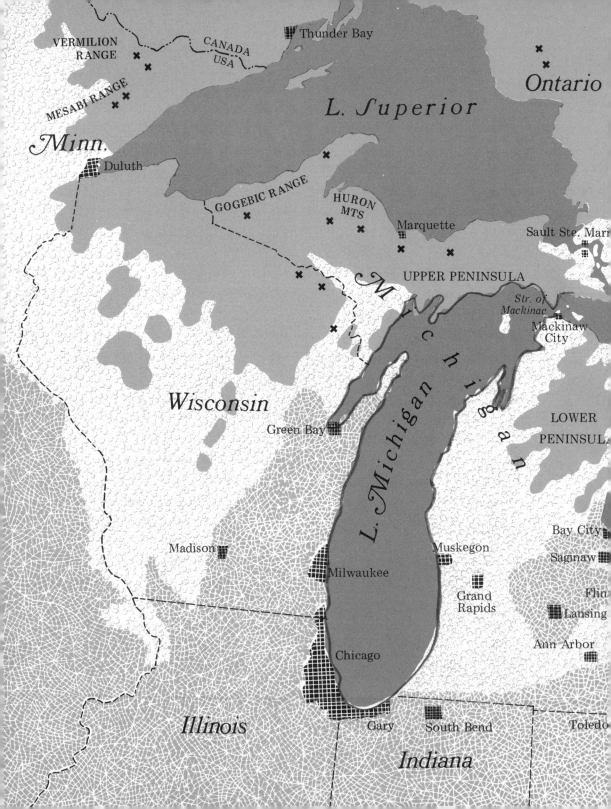

VERMILION RANGE

CANADA
USA

Thunder Bay

Ontario

MESABI RANGE

Minn.

L. Superior

Duluth

GOGEBIC RANGE

HURON MTS

Marquette

Sault Ste. Mari

UPPER PENINSULA

Str. of Mackinac

Mackinaw City

Wisconsin

Green Bay

M i c h i g a n

LOWER PENINSULA

L. Michigan

Bay City

Madison

Muskegon

Saginaw

Milwaukee

Grand Rapids

Flin

Lansing

Ann Arbor

Chicago

Illinois

Gary

South Bend

Toledo

Indiana

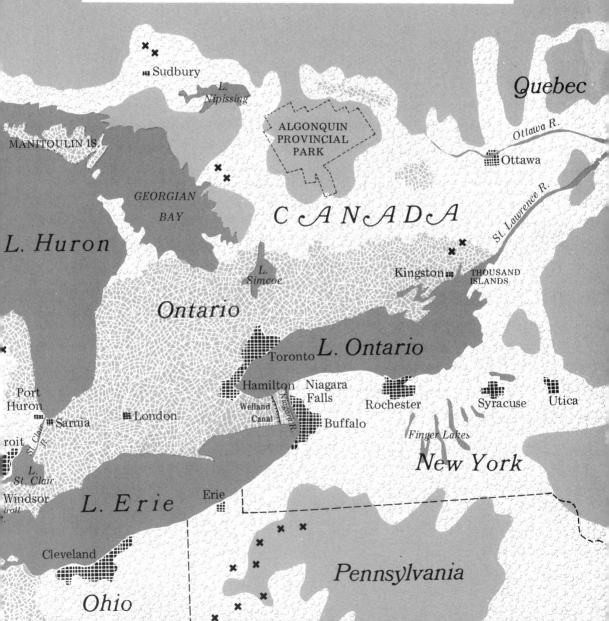

Economic map of the GREEN LAKES REGION

Economic map of the GREAT LAKES REGION

Built-up areas

Intensive farming land

Farming and woodland mixed

Woodland

✕ Mining

× ×
☷ Sudbury

L. Nipissing

MANITOULIN IS.

ALGONQUIN
PROVINCIAL
PARK

Quebec

Ottawa R.

☷ Ottawa

✕

GEORGIAN
BAY

C A N A D A

St. Lawrence R.

L. Huron

L. Simcoe

✕ ✕
Kingston ☷ THOUSAND
ISLANDS

Ontario

L. Ontario

✕

Toronto

Hamilton Niagara
Falls

Rochester

Syracuse Utica

Port
Huron

Welland
Canal

Niagara R.

Buffalo

Finger Lakes

roit *St. Clair R.* ☷ Sarnia ☷ London

New York

L.
St. Clair

Windsor
roit

L. Erie

Erie ☷

Pennsylvania

Cleveland

✕ ✕
✕ ✕

✕

Ohio

✕ ✕

THE GREAT LAKES

*A freighter being loaded
with grain, Lake Superior*

PASSING OVER
THE GREAT LAKES

A big ship named the *Red Wing* lies at a dock in the city of Duluth, Minnesota, at the western end of the Great Lakes. Tall ELEVATORS (buildings in which grain is stored) stand beside the ship. From one of them, wheat has run down through large pipes into the ship.

The cold morning wind is blowing in from Lake Superior, largest of the Great Lakes and the one farthest west. The sun has begun to come up. Loading of the ship has gone on all night; she is now full. (Ships have traditionally been referred to as feminine.) Workers are closing up the hatches, or openings, through which the ship has been loaded, making it ready to go out onto the lake.

Thirty minutes later the *Red Wing* heads out into open water, going under a lift bridge that rises slowly to let the ship pass and then lowers again behind her. The ship's long trip to the east has begun. In the next week she will go more than a thousand miles over the Great Lakes and then nearly another thousand along the Saint Lawrence River.

There are five Great Lakes. Four of them, Lakes Superior, Huron, Erie, and Ontario, lie between Canada and the United States. The ship, moving from west to east, will pass over these four in that order. Lake Ontario, the farthest east, runs into the Saint Lawrence River. Here the waters from the Great Lakes flow northeast to the Atlantic Ocean.

The fifth Great Lake, Lake Michigan, is all in the United States. It opens off Lake Huron and goes south for more than 300 miles. Lake Michigan is over 100 miles wide at its widest place. Ships also travel over the lake to cities on its shores, such as Milwaukee and Chicago.

The *Red Wing* first crosses Lake Superior. Other ships are also on the lake at this time. Some of them carry iron ore, the rock from which we get iron. Much iron ore is found around or near Lake Superior. It is being carried by ship to cities along the other Great Lakes, where it will go directly into large mills on the shores to be made into steel. (Steel is a metal used to make all kinds of things from cars to knives.) Other ships are bringing coal to cities on Lake Superior: to Duluth; to the city of Superior that lies next to it; to the city of Thunder Bay in Canada; and to other, smaller cities. These things that are carried by ships are known as FREIGHT, or CARGO, and so ships that carry freight are called FREIGHTERS.

Lake Superior is nearly 400 miles long and over 150 miles wide. Ships can pass over it and not see land for thirty hours at a time. In storms, waves can reach forty feet in height. But today as the *Red Wing* moves out onto the water the weather is good, the waves are not big, and the sun is shining. Water birds fly beside the ship. Off to the north lies Isle Royale, a large island that is now a national park. It has been kept in its natural state, and on it are wild animals such as gray wolves and moose. Now and again the *Red Wing* passes other ships. All day and all night she goes east, carrying her load of grain. As darkness comes, the ship's crew turn on the lights. This helps the crews of other ships see the *Red Wing* and tell which way she is going. Some of the crew sleep while others stay up to keep the ship moving during the night. The night crew will sleep later, when the others have awakened.

With morning approaching, the *Red Wing* nears the eastern end of Lake Superior. There, at a town with the French name of Sault Sainte Marie (usually just called "the Soo"), water from Lake Superior runs down to Lake Huron through the Saint Mary's River, dropping 24 feet as it goes. Because ships passing out of Lake Superior could be badly damaged if they tried to go through the quickly moving water of the Saint Mary's River, and ships going up into Lake Superior could not move at all against the strong press of river water, there is a CANAL to carry ships up or down between the two lakes. A canal is a man-made waterway. In this canal there are LOCKS. Locks look very much like huge boxes, open at the top and built into the ground. These "boxes" hold water, and each end of the lock has gates that, when closed, can keep water in or out.

The *Red Wing,* coming out of Lake Superior, moves through the open gates into a lock filled with water. This water is at the same level as that of Lake Superior and is held there by the closed gates at the other end of the lock. Once completely inside the lock, the *Red Wing* must wait while the gates at the Lake Superior end are shut so that they hold back Lake Superior water. Then the water in the lock is slowly let out through holes in its bottom. The freighter, riding on the water in the lock, slowly moves down with it. When the water in the lock is even with the water of Lake Huron,

HOW NAVIGATIONAL LOCKS WORK

These diagrams show how a ship is lowered in a lock. A ship is raised by reversing the operation. No pumps are required; the water is merely allowed to seek its own level.

With both UPPER GATES *and* LOWER GATES *closed, and with the* EMPTYING VALVE *closed and the* FILLING VALVE *open, the* LOCK CHAMBER *has been filled to the* UPPER LEVEL. *The* UPPER GATES *have then been opened, allowing the ship to enter the* LOCK CHAMBER.

Now the ship is in the LOCK CHAMBER. *The* UPPER GATES *and the* FILLING VALVE *have been closed, and the* EMPTYING VALVE *has been opened to allow water to flow from the* LOCK CHAMBER *to the* LOWER LEVEL.

The water level in the LOCK CHAMBER *has gone down to the* LOWER LEVEL, *the* LOWER GATES *have been opened, and the ship is leaving the* LOCK CHAMBER. *After this, the lock is ready for an upbound ship to come in and be lifted, or may be filled (as above) to lower another downbound ship.*

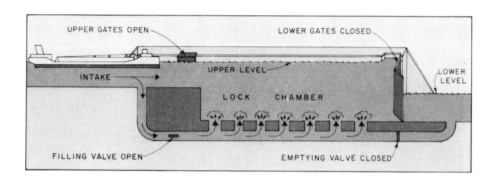

UPPER GATES OPEN — LOWER GATES CLOSED —

INTAKE →

UPPER LEVEL

LOWER LEVEL

LOCK   CHAMBER

FILLING VALVE OPEN — EMPTYING VALVE CLOSED

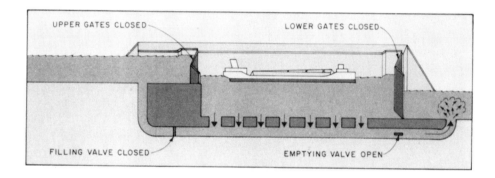

UPPER GATES CLOSED — LOWER GATES CLOSED —

FILLING VALVE CLOSED — EMPTYING VALVE OPEN

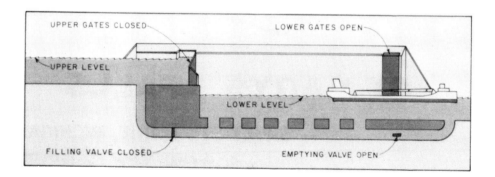

UPPER GATES CLOSED — LOWER GATES OPEN —

UPPER LEVEL

LOWER LEVEL

FILLING VALVE CLOSED — EMPTYING VALVE OPEN

*An overhead view of
the Soo's lock complex*

the gates at the Lake Huron end of the lock open, and the ship passes out of it at the lower level. At the same time, other ships in other locks are being lifted *up to* the level of Lake Superior.

Just below the locks, in the lower part of Saint Mary's River, where the water runs out to Lake Huron, our freighter meets many other ships. The canal at "the Soo" is one of the busiest in the world, and ships coming and going crowd the waters near it.

The rest of the day and the following night the *Red Wing* moves east and south through Lake Huron, the second largest Great Lake. Lake Huron is over 240 miles long and about 130 miles wide. Opening off the northern edge of Lake Huron are Georgian Bay and the North Channel. This is where the early French explorers first reached the Great Lakes. Today many people go there in summer to swim, boat, fish, and generally have fun outdoors. There are several small cities around Lake Huron, but no large ones. About the only things to see on the lake are other ships and birds, and the clouds or stars in the sky.

As morning comes again the ship moves into another crowded part of the system. (The Lakes themselves plus all the other waterways connected to them are called the GREAT LAKES SYSTEM.) This crowded part of the system is made up of the southern end of Lake Huron, the Saint Clair River that runs out of Lake Huron, Lake Saint Clair (a small lake that is part of the system but is not a Great Lake) into which the Saint Clair River runs, and the Detroit River that runs from Lake Saint Clair to Lake Erie. The water passing out of Lake Huron into Lake Erie runs south through the two rivers and Lake Saint Clair. Ships moving between Lakes Huron and Erie must also follow this same path. Our ship becomes one of a long line of freighters moving south, meeting another long line of them moving north. She passes many cities while traveling along the Detroit River, including Detroit on the American side and Windsor on the Canadian side.

Detroit, a city best known for its car manufacturing, is filled with factories and steel mills. Our ship passes Detroit in early afternoon. As she nears the city a MAIL BOAT, which meets all passing ships, comes up beside her. A crewman on the *Red Wing* lowers a pail on a line down to the mail boat. In it are letters the crew of the *Red Wing* has written. The man in the mail boat takes out the letters, which he will put into the U.S. Mail. He then places in the pail letters and newspapers for the people on the ship and turns his boat away as the crewman on the *Red Wing* pulls up the pail.

It is late afternoon when our ship moves out of the Detroit River into Lake Erie. She is passing north of the area in which British and American sailing ships fought the Battle of Lake Erie in 1813—the most important battle in the history of the Great Lakes. Lake Erie is 210 miles long and nearly 60 miles wide. It is the shallowest of the Great Lakes (only 210 feet deep at its deepest place, while Lake Superior, the deepest Great Lake, reaches over 1,300 feet at its deepest place). And because it is shallow, Lake Erie can be very dangerous in a storm, when the waves are short, move fast, and hit hard against ships. But the weather is good as the *Red Wing* turns east again and starts over Lake Erie. The sun is setting and the sky is turning dark. Stars are coming out.

Lake Erie is the dirtiest Great Lake because of the wastes

CANADIAN SHIELD

GREAT LAKES

PACIFIC RANGES

ROCKY MOUNTAINS

GREAT

PLAINS

APPALACHIAN HIGHLANDS

The
GREAT LAKES REGION

MINN.
Duluth

L. SUPERIOR

ST. LAWRENCE SEAWAY

Montreal

ONTARIO

MICHIGAN

WISCONSIN

L. MICHIGAN

L. HURON

Toronto

L. ONTARIO

NEW YORK

Buffalo

Detroit

L. St. Clair

L. ERIE

PENNSYLVANIA

Chicago
ILL.   INDIANA

OHIO

CROSS SECTION THROUGH
THE GREAT LAKES AND
ST. LAWRENCE SEAWAY

Duluth

Sault
Ste. Marie

L. St. Clair

Welland
Canal
(locks)

Montreal

L. SUPERIOR
600 ft above sea level

L. HURON 580ft

L. ERIE
570ft.

L. ONTARIO
250ft

(locks)

Sea level

St. Lawrence R.

*A freighter carrying grain from
Lake Superior to the Atlantic Ocean
passes the steel mills of Detroit.*

that pour into it from Detroit and other cities on the Detroit River and from the cities around Lake Erie. Many people live in the cities around Lake Erie, mostly south of the lake. The largest of these are Cleveland, which is about at the middle of the southern shore, and Buffalo, at the eastern end of the lake. Some of the other freighters that are coming out of the Detroit River ahead of our ship and behind her carry iron ore. They are heading farther south than the path the *Red Wing* is following, for they are taking their ore to the steel mills either of Cleveland or another Lake Erie city. But the *Red Wing* keeps moving east.

It is still dark but almost morning when the ship turns in toward the lights that mark a town called Port Colborne on the northeastern shore of the lake. Here is the beginning of another canal (called the Welland Canal) which runs through part of Canada. The Welland Canal starts at Port Colborne and takes ships down to the level of Lake Ontario. Its locks work the same way as those of the canal at Sault Sainte Marie. But instead of going through only one lock as she did to pass between Lakes Superior and Huron, here the ship must pass through eight locks that carry her down 326 feet.

Water runs from Lake Erie to Lake Ontario through the Niagara River, which goes between Canada and the United States. Before the water reaches Lake Ontario it must pass over Niagara Falls, dropping with a great noise as it falls the 326 feet. Of course ships cannot go this way, so the Welland Canal was built to take them around the falls.

The *Red Wing* is a ship of the largest size that can pass

through the locks of the Welland Canal. She is 730 feet long —nearly as long as two and a half football fields—and 75 feet wide. There are larger ships on the Great Lakes, the largest being 1,000 feet long and 105 feet wide. These ships usually carry iron ore from Lake Superior to steel mills on the shores of Lake Michigan or to other mills on the shores of Lake Erie. But the Welland Canal is not large enough to take them. So they must stay within the four lakes farthest west—Superior, Michigan, Huron, and Erie.

Three days and nights have passed since the *Red Wing* left Duluth with her cargo of grain. It will take another day for her to go through the eight locks of the Welland Canal, because many other ships are also going through in both directions, and she must wait her turn at each lock.

As the *Red Wing* leaves the Welland Canal and goes out into Lake Ontario, the sky is starting to darken. But the crew can still see the Canadian city of Toronto far away to their left. Toronto, capital of the province of Ontario, is the biggest Canadian city on the Great Lakes. It is not possible to see Toronto's shore, but the crew can see some of its tall buildings, which now look very small. They can also see the lights from the city shining into the evening sky. Now the ship turns east, and soon the buildings of Toronto can no longer be seen. Night falls. The ship moves on through the dark.

Lake Ontario is about 50 miles wide and 190 miles long. The dark night sky is just starting to turn gray. With the coming daylight the *Red Wing* passes the Canadian city of Kingston, off on the lake's northern shore, and enters the Saint Lawrence River. Duluth, where the ship was loaded with grain, is now 1,200 miles away, at the opposite end of the Great Lakes.

As morning comes the *Red Wing* moves through the Thousand Islands, the many small islands in the Saint Lawrence River. On these islands there are many summer homes, some farms, and several parks. Farther along the *Red Wing* moves through the seven locks of the Saint Lawrence Seaway, a part of the river that has been made into a canal so that ships can easily travel between the Great Lakes and the sea. Some of the other ships in the canal are ocean freighters, bringing cargo to the Lakes from faraway countries. They will pick up other cargoes at Great Lake cities and carry them back again across the ocean.

These locks in the Seaway take our freighter down another 200 feet. She goes through some of them during the night. Like all the other locks the ship has gone through, these locks work day and night. The area is brightly lighted at night so that the people who work the locks and the ships' crews can see. Shortly after daylight our ship leaves the locks behind and passes the city of Montreal, nearly 200 miles from Lake Ontario.

From there she goes another 500 miles down the river to the Canadian city of Port Cartier, on the edge of the Atlantic Ocean. There, at an elevator much like the one where she was originally loaded in Duluth a week ago, the *Red Wing* begins to unload her cargo. That same elevator will soon put the grain into an ocean freighter, a ship that is too large to pass through the locks of the Saint Lawrence Seaway and the Welland Canal. The ocean freighter will take the grain

overseas, where it may then be made into bread for the people of Europe or Africa.

The *Red Wing* now moves to another dock at Port Cartier. Here she will load iron ore that has come by train from northern Canada. In a day she will begin her journey back again to the Great Lakes, to a steel mill on the shore of Lake Michigan.

In the upper Saint Lawrence River
our ship, carrying grain, meets
another freighter bringing iron
ore to the Great Lakes.

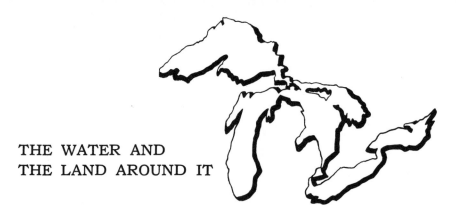

THE WATER AND
THE LAND AROUND IT

For thousands of years, during the period we call the Pleistocene Epoch, the land where the Great Lakes now lie was covered with a thick sheet of ice called a GLACIER. As a result of its great weight and movement, the glacier shaped the land below it, carving out valleys and other features. Then, very slowly, the air became warmer, and between fifteen and twenty thousand years ago the ice, which was several hundred feet thick, began to melt. As the glacier turned to water, its southern edge very slowly pulled back north. The melted ice formed lakes and rivers along the glacier's edge. But during the thousands of years when the ice was melting, the air was not always warm. Sometimes, for several hundred years at a time, it would turn cold again, causing the glacier to grow larger and again move south. Then once more the air would become warm, and once more the glacier would begin to melt and move north. Because of this, in some places the glacier not only left lakes and rivers behind as it melted, but it also came back again and again to change their size and shape.

Glacial markings left in the limestone
rock on Kelleys Island in Lake Erie

About ten thousand years ago the edge of the glacier at last moved north into Canada, leaving a lot of water where the Great Lakes are now. At that time there was much more water in the Lakes than there is today. But in time much of the water ran off into the Mississippi, Hudson, and Saint Lawrence rivers, and into some rivers that no longer even exist. Only about two thousand years ago the Great Lakes began to look something like they do now.

Because of the back and forth movement of the glacier, and because the Lakes themselves grew smaller and smaller after the glacier disappeared altogether, today we can see clearly marked on the land places where old shorelines, lake-beds, and riverbeds were.

As the Lakes slowly dropped to their present size, the water became too low to run off through most of the rivers it had once followed. Today the water in all of the Lakes runs toward only one river, the Saint Lawrence. (Some of the water in Lake Michigan flows into a canal at Chicago, which carries it to the Mississippi River System.) From the time the extra water from the glacier ran off to the oceans, the Lakes have stayed about the same size because of snow and rainfall. Sometimes there will be a lot of rain and snow, and for a few years the waters of the Great Lakes will be high on their shores. Then, for several more years, there may not be much rain and snow, and the level of the Lakes will drop lower.

Of all the Lakes, Superior holds the most water—so much that it takes 190 years for the lake to empty and re-fill itself again. (Of course new water runs in as old water runs out, so the lake is always filled with water.) Lake Michigan takes 100 years to empty and refill, Huron 20 years, Ontario 8 years, and Erie only 3 years.

The weather around the Great Lakes is cold in winter and hot in summer. In winter, it gets so cold that lake water freezes at many points, and special ships, called ICEBREAKERS, have to cut paths through the ice. In summer, the air over much of the Great Lakes countryside is hot. Because water temperature changes more slowly than air temperature, the water during the summer stays colder than the air. These conditions allow beach-goers to enjoy a cool dip in the water.

When water changes temperature more slowly than that of the land and air around it, however, stormy weather may result. In summer, hot winds blowing across one of the Lakes may draw up the cooler water and then drop it as heavy rain on some of the cities along the shores. In winter, much the same thing happens when dry, cold winds pick up warmer water from one of the Lakes—but what they drop then is snow. Five feet of snow may pile up in only a few hours at Gary, Indiana; Cleveland, Ohio; or Oswego, New York. But the worst storms that strike the Great Lakes start west of the Lakes themselves and move east toward them. They hit most often during fall and winter.

The worst storm ever recorded on the Lakes, known as the "Big Blow," took place over four days in 1913. It was made up of three separate storms all coming together at once over the Lakes. During the "Big Blow" 19 ships were destroyed and 20 others went aground. Over 250 people were killed. Ten of the ships were lost on Lake Huron, five on

*Here, at one o'clock in the
morning, iron ore is being
loaded into a freighter on the
northern shore of Lake Superior.*

Lake Superior, three on Lake Michigan, and one on Lake Erie. The one lost on Erie was a LIGHTSHIP, a ship designed to meet the worst possible weather and anchored in open water to act as a guide for other ships. Several of the vessels lost were ocean freighters working on the Lakes. Meanwhile, snow, rain, and wind were hitting the shores of the Lakes, blocking roads and rail lines, sweeping away buildings near the water's edge, and even blowing people into the waves where they drowned.

Many minerals used by industry are found in the land around the Great Lakes, the most important one being iron ore. More than two thirds of all the iron ore in the United States is gotten from the Great Lakes area. Most of it comes from around Lake Superior, but some is also found along the northwestern shore of Lake Michigan and north of Lake Huron.

Among the other minerals found in the Great Lakes area are the metals zinc, lead, silver, and copper, all of which are deposited only in the oldest rock formations. These rocks are around most of Lake Superior, north of Lake Huron, and at the eastern end of Lake Ontario. At other places around the Lakes there are small deposits of coal and larger amounts of gas and oil. The gas and oil are mainly in Michigan, Ontario, and Pennsylvania. Such rocks as dolomite, sandstone, shale, gypsum, and salt, come from many places around the Lakes. They are also important minerals and are used in a number of different things from building houses to seasoning food. In addition, such useful minerals as sand and gravel, clay, marl, and peat are found in the area.

THE HISTORY

Ten thousand years ago there were people living around the huge glacial lakes that slowly turned into the Great Lakes. These early people, American Indians, lived mostly by hunting animals. They ate the meat of the animals, made clothing from the skins, and used the bones for tools.

For nearly ten thousand years these early American Indians were the only people to know the Great Lakes. Then, not quite 400 years ago, a French boy named Étienne Brûlé came to the Lakes. By that time three major Indian peoples were living there. The Algonkian Indians lived mostly north of Lake Superior, Lake Huron, Lake Ontario, and the Saint Lawrence River, although small bands of them lived in other places as well. The Iroquoian Indians lived mostly east of Lake Huron, around Lake Erie, and south of Lake Ontario and the Saint Lawrence River. The Siouxian Indians lived mostly west of Lake Michigan and north of Lake Superior, although a few of them lived south of Lake Ontario.

Each of these peoples was broken into many smaller groups, called tribes. But most of the tribes within a particular grouping of peoples spoke much the same language.

The Algonkians lived mostly by hunting and fishing. The Iroquoians hunted and fished, but they also grew corn, beans, and other food, and tobacco to smoke. The Siouxian were also both farmers and hunters. Some who lived west of Lake Michigan moved farther west each year, away from the Great Lakes, to hunt buffalo. These animals were wanted for meat and for skins by many of the Indians who lived on the western plains.

Most Great Lakes Indians used a type of boat called a CANOE, made from the bark of a birch tree. These birchbark canoes were light and easy to use on the rivers that run into the Great Lakes. They could easily be lifted out of the water and carried past the RAPIDS (parts of a river where the current runs fast and the surface is broken by rocks). The canoes could also be used on the Great Lakes themselves, but there the Indians had to stay close to shore so that if a storm came up they could reach land before the waters grew too dangerous. Since there were no roads at that time, the Indians went nearly everywhere by canoe.

The Indian tribes who traveled the Great Lakes by canoe naturally made up stories about voyages on the Lakes. One story explains how Nanabazhoo, a Chippewa spirit (the Chippewas were a tribe of the Algonkian peoples who lived on the shores of Lake Superior) brought his people fire to keep them warm in winter. He built a bark canoe and paddled eastward across the Great Lakes until he came to a land where an old man who had fire lived with his two daughters. They guarded the fire so carefully that no one could steal it. Nanabazhoo turned himself into a hare. When the girls came out of their wigwam they saw the little bunny sitting there, wet and shivering. They picked him up, took him inside, and put him down near the fire. The old man was asleep and the girls were busy. The little bunny hopped nearer the fire. Then he grabbed a stick of burning wood and ran back to his canoe, in which he quickly paddled away. The old man and his daughters chased him but could not catch him. While the hare was carrying the fire, sparks from it fell on his fur and burned him. That, according to the story, is why the fur of the hare turns from white to brown each year.

Many years later the poet Henry W. Longfellow changed Nanabazhoo's name to Hiawatha and wrote a long poem about him. In the poem Longfellow retold many of the stories about Lake Superior. He used the Indian name for it, Gitchee Goomee, meaning "Great Water," and described the different shores of the lake, from the sand hills to the colored cliffs called the Pictured Rocks.

In 1609, some Huron Indians, a tribe of Iroquoians living southeast of Georgian Bay on Lake Huron, set out in their canoes on a long trip. They went to see the strange white-skinned tribe they heard had come to live on the lower part of the Saint Lawrence River. These white people were the French, and they had named the area in which they had settled Quebec. The Hurons canoed from Georgian Bay through rivers and small lakes to the Ottawa River. Then they went down the Ottawa and Saint Lawrence till they met the French near Quebec. On this trip there were thirty-five places where they had to carry their canoes past the rapids or travel across country between rivers and lakes— sometimes for as much as six miles at a time. It took the Hurons between three and four weeks to reach the French.

The Hurons found that the French would trade iron tools

and other useful things for animal skins, especially the skins of beavers. Since large numbers of beaver were easily gotten from the rivers and smaller lakes around the Great Lakes, the Hurons were able to trade for the things they wanted. They also wanted the French to help them in their wars against other tribes. So they returned to Quebec the next year. And that year the French sent back with them an eighteen-year-old boy, Étienne Brûlé. Thus Étienne became the first white person to see the Great Lakes. It was the year 1610.

Over the next hundred years various Frenchmen explored every part of the Great Lakes and beyond them, most of the time riding in birchbark canoes. One of the first of these explorers was Samuel de Champlain, governor of the colony of New France, based at Quebec. In 1615, Champlain came to the Great Lakes, following the Ottawa River and other rivers to Georgian Bay—the same way Brûlé had come earlier. Champlain called Georgian Bay *La Mer Douce,* which means "the Freshwater Sea." He came there to the country of the Huron Indians who, when they visited Quebec, had asked him to help them in a war against their enemies, the Iroquois, who lived in what is now northern New York. He and a few other Frenchmen went by canoe with an army of Hurons over small lakes and streams to Lake Ontario. Then they went along that lake to its eastern end where it flows into the Saint Lawrence River—where, Champlain said, there were "very large, beautiful islands"—and south to Lake Oneida.

There they attacked an Iroquois village. In the fight, seventeen Hurons were wounded. This discouraged the Hurons so much that they stopped the attack, waited nearby for several days, and then started back home. Champlain wanted them to attack again, but they would not. Because his knee and leg had been hurt in the fight, Champlain had to be carried to the canoes. He went back to Georgian Bay with the Hurons, and there spent the winter. The following May he returned to Quebec.

Champlain never came to the Great Lakes again, but he sent other men. Brûlé was probably the first to explore Lake Superior, in 1618. In 1634, Jean Nicolet, looking for a way to reach China, went as far as Green Bay, Wisconsin. After Champlain's death other Frenchmen came to the Lakes. Two brothers-in-law named Radisson and Grosseilliers traveled over them and became the first white people to canoe on the upper Mississippi River. Adrien Jolliet in 1669 went out to Lake Superior, then returned by way of Lake Erie. Though Brûlé may have been the first to see Lake Erie, Jolliet was the first to tell about it. In 1673, Jolliet and the missionary Father Jacques Marquette started out from Lake Michigan, crossed to the Mississippi, and went down it as far as the mouth of the Arkansas River.

But one of the greatest explorers of the area was René Robert Cavelier, Sieur de la Salle—usually just called La Salle. He came to Canada in 1666, when he was twenty-three years old. Over the next ten years he explored the Ohio Valley and the Great Lakes as far as the southern shore of Lake Michigan. He probably also went on to Lake Superior. Between 1673 and 1677, he built Fort Frontenac at the eastern end of Lake Ontario and brought fifty to sixty French people to live there. During this time he returned twice to France to get help from the French king. La Salle had the first ships to sail the Great Lakes built at Fort Frontenac. These were very small sailing vessels. We do not know the exact years when they were built, but at least two of them were in use by 1678.

In 1678 and 1679, La Salle had a ship built on the upper part of the Niagara River. He called this ship the *Griffon*. She was the first ship ever to sail on Lake Erie, Lake Huron, and Lake Michigan, passing over all of them in August of 1679. But on the return trip that September she disappeared and never was seen again. La Salle, however, continued to use the Great Lakes as the starting place for other explorations. In 1681 and 1682, he went over the Lakes and down the Mississippi River to its mouth on the Gulf of Mexico. There he claimed for France the area we now call Louisiana.

Over the years the French wanted the Indians to live much as they always had, to hunt animals such as the beaver and to trade the animal furs with them. The furs were then sent by canoe to Quebec and from there by ship back over the ocean to France. French people who traded for the furs lived at different places around the Great Lakes, but they did not build big towns or cities on the Lakes. The only people they brought there were those few men who had business (and sometimes their families).

But during this same period, many British people were coming across the ocean to live in America on the edge of the Atlantic. One of the cities they built there, New York, was only about 200 miles from Lake Ontario. Other British cities along the Atlantic were farther away from the Great Lakes. Many of the British who had come to America wanted land they could farm. So in time they began to move farther in from the coast, buying or just taking land from the Indians, cutting down trees, and setting up farms. This was quite different from what the French had done.

The French continued to hold the land around and south of the Great Lakes, even though the British felt they had a right to it. France and Great Britain were already at war, and before long they were fighting over this land too. Because many Indians fought on the side of the French, this series of battles is called the French and Indian Wars (1754–1763). The French were defeated by 1760 in spite of Indian help. This happened mainly because the French government was less interested in this part of the world than the British and refused to send over much help.

After the fighting ended in 1760, Britain sent soldiers to stay at many places around the Lakes where the French had lived and traded for furs. But the British did not treat the Indians as well as the French had, and in 1763 the Indian tribes led by Pontiac, one of the greatest Indian chiefs of all time, rose up in what was called Pontiac's Rebellion. The Indians killed British settlers and soldiers all around the Lakes area, except in Detroit and Niagara, which were too heavily protected for the Indians to take.

By this time the Indians had grown used to having the things they had traded for with the French—iron tools, guns, and gunpowder, for example. But the British refused to trade with the Indians while the fighting was going on. Instead of supplies they were sending over only more and more soldiers to fight. After two more years of fighting the Indians saw that they had to make peace with the British, and they did.

With Pontiac's Rebellion over, British leaders in England

wanted to get along better with the Indians. So they made a law forbidding the British people to settle in the country around the Great Lakes and south of it. Many men and women living in British cities along the American shore of the Atlantic Ocean had wanted to settle Indian country. To make sure the people did not move into that area, the British government put soldiers in many cities where the people lived. The people did not like this, and it was one of several reasons why they freed themselves from British rule in the American Revolution (1775–1783).

There was little fighting around the Great Lakes during the American Revolution. After it was over, people who still wanted to be British moved to Canada. Many Americans living in the eastern parts of the country, however, began to move west. But the British in Canada still thought the land around the Great Lakes and south of them should be Indian country. So they helped the Indians fight the ever-growing numbers of Americans moving west and taking over land to turn it into farms.

Much fighting took place between the settlers and the Indians until 1794, when an army of soldiers led by the American Revolutionary War leader General Anthony Wayne fought the Indians near the eastern end of Lake Erie, at a place where a storm had blown over many trees. In this battle, known as the Battle of Fallen Timbers, the Americans

Over: Pontiac, the great Indian leader, is depicted here parleying with British settlers.

The U.S. brig Niagara, *as she breaks through the British line during the Battle of Lake Erie. This picture was painted by Charles A. Patterson and Howard B. French for the U.S. Naval Academy Museum.*

won, and the Indians then made peace with them. After that, American settlement could begin along the southern shores of the Great Lakes.

In the early 1800s another war broke out between the British and Americans, the War of 1812. During it there was fighting between sailing ships on Lakes Ontario, Erie, and Huron. Soldiers also fought along the shores of these Lakes.

The most important battle ever to take place on the Great Lakes occurred during the War of 1812. It took place on Lake Erie, and is thus known as the Battle of Lake Erie. In it, groups of sailing ships from both sides fought on September 10, 1813. The American naval commander was Oliver Hazard Perry. When his own ship, the *Lawrence,* became too badly damaged to fight, he had himself rowed in a small boat through the middle of the battle to another ship in his command, the *Niagara.* Taking over the *Niagara,* he headed her straight for the British line of ships. He broke through it, firing his cannon to both sides as he went, and soon won the battle. Shortly afterward Perry sent the famous message to army commander General William Henry Harrison: "We have met the enemy and they are ours."

After the War of 1812 was over, people on both the American and Canadian sides of the Great Lakes began to settle along the shores, and the cities we know today began to grow.

FUN ON THE LAKES

There are many ways people enjoy the Great Lakes in their free time. Some who like to sightsee visit the many attractions of the larger cities on the shores. Others visit historical sites in the Lakes area. There are old forts that show how people lived and fought in times past. The sailing ship that was rebuilt after it was used in the Battle of Lake Erie is now on display in Erie, Pennsylvania. The lighthouses (towers with lights on top) that were built to help guide ships at night are worth seeing. And you can visit the birthplace of the inventor Thomas A. Edison.

But those who want to be more active—or just want to spend time away from the crowded cities to relax with nature —also head for the Great Lakes. The shores of the Lakes are often very different. At some places there are sand beaches. At other places there are DUNES, big hills of sand that sometimes move or change shape when a strong wind blows. At still other places high rock cliffs come straight down to the water. And there are places where one can find marks left by glaciers or small lakes that were scooped out by the glaciers. The northern shores of Lakes Huron and Superior are made up of some of the oldest rock in the world. The rock of these shores is rounded and not very high in most places, but it is very hard. Trees grow there but not many other plants. This happens because there is not much earth on the rocks for the plants to grow in. And because these rocks are so hard it is not easy to build roads or even houses on them. Fewer people live there than on most of the other shores.

Of course the Lakes offer all sorts of water and beach sports, including fishing, swimming, and boating. Because of the different ways the shores meet the water, it is easier to swim, sail, canoe, or fish at some places than at others. One may also golf or play tennis, go horseback riding or bicycling in the Lakes area.

Campers and nature lovers also flock to the Lakes to observe and enjoy the variety of plant and animal life. Fortunately there are still unsettled areas, some of which have been made into parks for campers and wildlife observers to use.

Because of the great distances the Great Lakes cover, many different kinds of plants and animals can live around them. Most of the plants growing on the rocky shores north of Lake Superior are different from those growing in the marshes south of Lake Erie. To the north of the Lakes grow certain evergreen trees—spruce, jack pine, balsam. South of these trees are maple and beech. Then comes an area in which such trees as birch and poplar mix with other kinds of evergreens like white pine and hemlock. But these are only general rules. For the woodlands change not only from north to south but also according to the kinds of soil. Some trees grow best in dry soil, others in swamps. Some need certain chemicals in the soil. The smaller plants follow the same kinds of complicated patterns. For example, the Alaska orchid grows

A beach on Georgian Bay

in the Great Lakes region only on the Bruce Peninsula, between Georgian Bay and Lake Huron, the only place where it can get all the things it needs to live.

Fish of many kinds live in the waters of the Lakes. People have fished there ever since the first Indians came. In more recent years, some kinds of fish that used to be plentiful have decreased in number because too many of them were caught or because people changed the water conditions, usually by making the water dirty. Some kinds of Great Lakes fish have been killed by the SEA LAMPREY, an animal that looks like an eel and has sharp teeth. It came into the Lakes from the ocean, either by way of the Saint Lawrence River or the Hudson River and the canals that connect the Hudson to the Great Lakes. Recently state and provincial governments around the Lakes have spent a great deal of money to get rid of the lampreys. They are not now as big a problem as they were.

Today the fish most often used for human food are yellow perch, chub, white bass, whitefish, walleye, smelt, and lake trout. There are also very large numbers of carp, alewife, suckers, and sheepshead, but they are used less often for human food. Because conditions in each of the Lakes are different, each lake contains more of some kinds of fish than of others. For instance, large, deep, cold Lake Superior has many herring, trout, and whitefish, while shallow, dirty Lake Erie has many yellow perch, sheepshead, and carp.

The land animals that live around the Great Lakes also vary greatly, because the Lakes cover such a wide region. There are still gray wolves and moose in some of the areas north of Lake Superior and in Isle Royale National Park, which lies just off the northern shore of that lake. Black bears and beavers are found along the more northern shores of the Great Lakes. On the Canadian shores of Lakes Superior and Huron, linxes and bobcats can still occasionally be seen. By contrast, on the southern shores of Lake Erie we find musk-rats, opossums, and rabbits. There are porcupines in the wilder places around the Lakes and racoons everywhere. White-tailed deer can also be found all around, even in the farmlands between the cities of Lake Erie. And many kinds of small animals live on every shore, such as squirrels, mice, moles, and skunks.

The fish and land animals of the Great Lakes region do not travel far. They usually spend their lives in one area. But most of the birds come and go. As the weather becomes warmer in the spring, great numbers of birds fly north from places far to the south. Some of them spend the warm weather months on the Lakes. Others fly across the Great Lakes and go much farther north. Then, as the weather grows colder in the autumn, the birds from the north fly across the Great Lakes again, heading south. And most of the birds that spent the summer on the Lakes go south with them.

Because birds go north in summer and south in winter, and because so many of the birds going to and coming from the far north fly across the Lakes, at times one can see many different kinds in this region. One of the places where the traveling birds stop is Point Pelee on the Canadian shore of Lake Erie. In spring more than a hundred species of birds will stop there to rest and eat before flying on. Among the water birds that spend the summer on the Lakes are gulls, terns, ducks, sandpipers, and herons. In recent summers American egrets have come as far north as Lake Erie. And birds as different as robins, woodpeckers, and eagles live around the shores in summer.

SHIPS, SHIPPING,
AND SHIPBUILDING

History

The first white people to come to the Great Lakes traveled by birchbark canoes they themselves built or got from the Indians. As late as the 1870s, some canoes were still used for carrying people and cargoes, mostly along the Canadian shore. But shipbuilding began on the Lakes much earlier. At first only sailing ships were built, but soon after the War of 1812 people began building steamships, and by 1900 steamers carried most of the cargoes.

With the passing of years, freighters have grown larger and larger. In 1874, the largest ship on the Lakes, the *V.H. Ketchum,* was so big—233 feet long—she could not even enter many harbors of that day. Now Great Lakes shipbuilders are building freighters 1,000 feet long, but of course the harbors are much larger today. A number of smaller ships are still being built to do various jobs, but none of them is nearly as small as the *Ketchum.*

The Cargoes the Ships Carry

Today there are about 300 lake freighters. They carry mostly iron ore, coal, and grain. Most of the iron ore (the leading cargo) is brought from ports on Lake Superior and northern Lake Michigan to ports on Lake Erie and southern Lake Michigan. Some of it is carried from Saint Lawrence River ports through the Seaway to Lake Erie or Lake Michigan ports. And some goes to Canadian steel mills at Sault Sainte Marie and at the city of Hamilton on Lake Ontario.

Coal ranks second as the Lakes' most important cargo. Most of it goes from Lake Erie cities to other ports on the Lakes, to steel mills, factories, and electric power plants. Many of the ships carrying coal are built to unload themselves. These ships are known as SELF-UNLOADERS. There are about seventy-five self-unloaders on the Lakes, carrying coal, stone, and iron ore.

Grain ranks third on the list. It is shipped out of Thunder Bay, Duluth and Superior, Chicago, and a few other ports. Most of it travels through the Saint Lawrence Seaway on lake freighters to ports on the lower Saint Lawrence River or on the Atlantic Ocean, where it is then put into ocean freighters. Some goes directly overseas by ocean freighters that load at Great Lake ports.

Yet another important cargo on the Great Lakes is oil or oil products such as gasoline. It is carried in ships called TANKERS. There are about forty tankers on the Lakes. Most of them carry oil products, loading them at the ports where they are manufactured and taking them to ports where they either are used or are put on trucks and trains that carry them overland to users in other cities and towns.

Ocean ships, coming from or going to ports overseas, carry about a quarter of the cargo that moves through the Saint Lawrence Seaway. They bring to the Great Lakes things such

Above left: a freighter carrying iron ore from Lake Superior to steel mills on the other Lakes. Below left: the self-unloader shown here is carrying crushed rock. Above: a Great Lakes tanker, carrying oil or gasoline, moves through a narrow passage among the islands of Georgian Bay.

as cars made in other countries, food, and toys. They may carry out of the Lakes grain or scrap iron (used pieces of iron to be melted down and used again) or almost any of the products that are made by factories of the Lakes' cities. Most of the big ports on the Great Lakes load and unload ocean freighters as well as lake freighters.

The Modern
Lake Freighters

Each lake ship has a crew of about thirty people, who do everything from steering the ship to cooking the meals. The people in charge of the ship are the ship's officers. First in rank is the captain. The officers who help the captain are called mates. Each ship also has a chief engineer, helped by assistant engineers, who looks after the ship's engines.

Both Canada and the United States have schools to train young people to be ships' officers, such as Georgian College, Owen Sound, in Canada and Northwestern Michigan College, Traverse City, Michigan, in the United States. Another way to become an officer on a ship is to start as a sailor and work up through the ranks. In past years, when there were no schools, this was the only way to advance.

Building a lake freighter costs from $15 million to $35 million. A ship's cargo may be worth several million dollars. So the captains and other officers of these ships must be well-trained. Ships can run into each other in crowded waters, can hit underwater rocks, and can go down in storms. Almost every year one or two ships are lost on the Great Lakes.

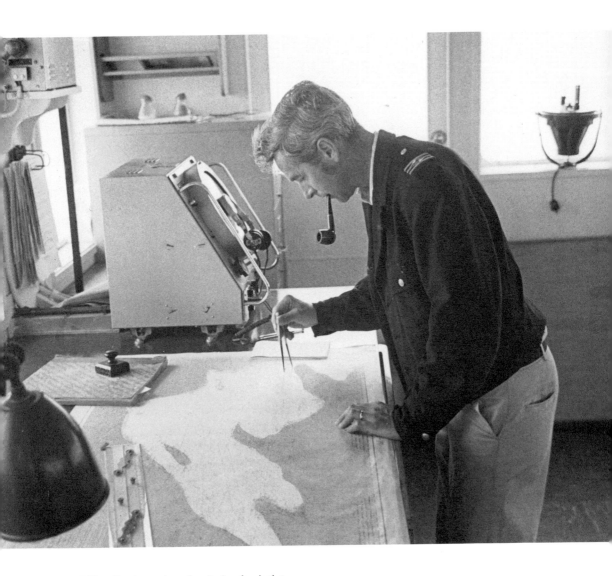

The first mate of a lake freighter
plots his ship's position on Lake Superior.

In a year a lake freighter may make thirty or more trips carrying iron ore from the western end of Lake Superior to Lake Erie or Lake Michigan ports. It may make just as many trips going back to Lake Superior again. Ships carrying coal over shorter distances will make more trips. Ships carrying grain over the longer distance through the Saint Lawrence Seaway will not make as many trips.

In cold weather, parts of the Great Lakes turn to ice. At one time this kept ships from moving during the three or four coldest months of each year. But now, many things are being done to help freighters move in winter. Icebreakers break the ice up so that the freighters can get through. In some places air is piped to the bottom of the lake, causing bubbles to rise to the top; this keeps ice from forming, and ships can then easily move over those areas. Now each year some freighters keep on working well into the winter months.

Cargo ships use less fuel than other ways of moving freight. Trains use more than two times as much to carry the same cargo, and trucks use over eleven times as much. So if it were not for the ships of the Great Lakes, everything they carry would cost more. As one example, steel made from iron ore would cost more, and because of that the products made from steel, such as cars, would also cost more.

POLLUTION

One of the greatest problems facing the Great Lakes today is POLLUTION. When water is polluted it is dirty, and now many parts of the Great Lakes are dirty. It is bad to swim or boat in places where the water is polluted, and fish often get sick and die in large numbers because of polluted waters.

A number of different things cause water pollution. One of the chief ones is human waste (sewage). In some places human wastes are just run into the water without anything being done to them. But most cities put these wastes through SEWAGE TREATMENT PLANTS. These plants treat the wastes in order to make them less harmful to put into the water. Some of the plants just break up the wastes and let the heavy parts settle before they run what is left into the lake. The better plants also clean up the wastes so that they neither smell bad nor carry disease. But even these cleaner wastes hurt the Lakes, because they act as food for a very small water plant called ALGA (pl. algae), causing it to grow in the Lakes in great numbers. Algae in a lake can grow so thick that boats have a hard time moving through. And people stay away from areas along the shore where algae are growing. Living for only a brief time, algae when they die give off a really bad smell. Dead algae out in the open Lakes are a much more

Left: algae growing along a rocky shore.
Above: at Cleveland, the dirty water
in the harbor—the water nearest us in
the picture—flows out into the cleaner
water of Lake Erie beyond.

On another day, from another angle,
the dirty water flowing out of
Cleveland harbor looks black.

serious hazard. They fall to the bottom, and as they rot, they take oxygen out of the water. Fish in these areas often smother to death.

In our homes today we use soaps, called DETERGENTS, to clean clothes and other things. After these detergents are used, they are washed away with the waste water. They go into sewage treatment plants, and, in many cases, straight through them into the Lakes. Detergents contain PHOSPHATE, which is good food for algae. One pound of phosphate can grow a thousand pounds of algae. So in the last few years, as more and more detergents have been used, more and more algae have grown in the Lakes. Now, at a huge cost, most sewage treatment plants are being changed so that they can remove detergents from the wastes.

Factories may also put wastes into the water. Sometimes they take water from the Lakes for use in making their products, but when they put it back it is not as clean as when they took it out. Some years ago factories put wastes containing the element mercury into the Lakes. Mercury taken into the body can cause sickness and even death. The mercury got into some kinds of fish, and people had to stop eating these fish. Although these factories no longer put mercury into the water, in some places there is still a lot of it present that sank to the bottom. Fish feeding in those areas still cannot be eaten. And this is only one of the harmful things factories have put into the Lakes.

Farmers cause pollution too. When they plow the earth, turning it over so that they can plant seeds, some of that earth gets washed away by rain. The earth goes into rivers,

Left: a paper mill at Erie, Pennsylvania, pours wastes into Lake Erie, making a black cloud in the water along the shore. Lake Erie is the most polluted Great Lake. Above: fish, killed by water pollution, have been washed up on shore.

which then carry it to the Lakes. At first the earth dirties the water, and then sinks to the bottom. In some areas so much earth has piled up on the bottom of the Lakes that the water has become too shallow, and ships called DREDGES have to dig out the dirt so that other ships can get through. Farmers also add FERTILIZERS to their soil to feed their growing plants. But some of the fertilizers wash away and end up in the Lakes, where they feed the algae instead. Lastly, farmers also put INSECTICIDES (chemicals to kill insects) on their plants to kill any bugs that might eat the plants. The rain washes some of these chemicals into the water, where they get into the fish. When birds eat the fish, the insecticides get into the birds' eggs, and the eggs will not hatch. Thus, some of the species of birds that have always lived around the Lakes are dying out.

The people all around the Great Lakes now know about the pollution problems. To stop pollution, however, costs a lot of money, and so we are moving only very slowly to that end. But while the total amount needed to clean up the Great Lakes seems very large, if you break down the actual cost into the amount each one of the millions of people who live around the Lakes would have to pay, it does not seem so much. At most, it would cost about the same as a person would have to pay for food to eat for two or three days. It is possible to clean up the Great Lakes, if we want to.

LET'S PUT IT
ALL TOGETHER

The Great Lakes cover 94,560 square miles, more area than any other body of fresh water in the world. Lake Superior is the largest of them. Lakes Huron, Michigan, Erie, and Ontario follow in size in that order. But while Lake Huron covers more surface area than Lake Michigan, Lake Michigan is deeper and holds more water; and while Erie covers more surface than Ontario, Ontario is deeper and holds more water. From the northern tip of the Lakes to the southern tip the distance is about 500 miles, and from west to east about 800 miles. (But you can see from the map that ships traveling over the Lakes must go much farther in order to get from one end to the other.) About 40 million people live in the Great Lakes area.

All of the Great Lakes are far above sea level. Superior lies 600 feet above; Michigan and Huron, 578 feet; Erie, 570 feet; and Ontario, 245 feet. Because of the canals and locks, however, ships can pass between all of the Lakes and go down the Saint Lawrence River to the sea.

The water level of the Lakes depends on the amount of rain and snow falling around and into them. A little more rain and snow fall at the eastern end of the system (about 34 inches into Ontario) than at the western end (about 29 inches into Superior) during the year. Nearly two-thirds of this water goes back into the air again by turning into a gas form— WATER VAPOR. The other third runs off through the Lakes System and the Saint Lawrence River.

The level of the Lakes changes from year to year, depending on the amount of rain and snowfall. The level also changes by one or two feet during the year; usually it is highest in the summer and lowest in late winter. But storms and winds can change the level at any one place for a short time. Such changes happen most often in Lake Erie, the shallowest of the group. Storms can sometimes bring high waves into the streets of Lake Erie towns. At times the difference in water level between one end of Lake Erie and the other has been 13½ feet.

The exact shape of all the Lakes is always slowly changing. The earth under them rises along some shores and sinks along others between one and two feet every 100 years. Waves, too, can change the shape of the shores during a storm. The changes occur most quickly and can be seen most easily around Lake Erie. This is because Erie is the shallowest lake and because many of its shores are made up of sand or gravel, material that waves can easily cut into. But the same thing happens to some extent around all of the Great Lakes.

Materials produced or used near the Great Lakes, such as iron ore and coal, are shipped over the Lakes in freighters. The Great Lakes System is also used for moving cargoes between many places far from the Lakes, because it is easier and cheaper to use than any other route. The most important such cargo is the wheat that comes by train from northern United States and western Canada, which is then shipped

Weather conditions help change the
exact shape of the Lakes. Here stormy
winter weather is causing trees to
fall. The ice forming along the shore
is cutting into the shoreline.

across the Great Lakes to ports all over the world. More cargo goes through the canal at Sault Sainte Marie—"the Soo"—than through any other canal on the American continents except the Panama Canal, and in some years more cargo has gone through the Soo than through the Panama. The ports of the Great Lakes often handle more cargo during a year than those of the United States Pacific Coast and Gulf Coast put together.

Over the past hundred years, as more and more people have come to live in the Great Lakes area, the water in the Lakes has become dirtier and dirtier. People have poured all kinds of things into the water. The things that have caused the most harm are human wastes, detergents, and the run-off from farms. Each provides food for the healthy lake's enemy, algae. Other things that have caused problems are insecticides and factory wastes. These may get into fish and then may harm animals or people who eat the fish. Or pollutants may make the drinking water unsafe. Where the water has been polluted, the Lakes are not good for swimming or boating. Further, treatment of drinking water is more difficult and more expensive. And, finally, fish die in large numbers or absorb dangerous wastes and cannot be eaten. To save the Lakes we must stop polluting them now.

INDEX